D0485659

THE

GUIDE TO
PHILADELPHIA

Eileen Ogintz

Globe
Pequot

Guilford, Connecticut

Thank you to the students and teachers at Overbrook Elementary School;
to Mel Yemma for fact checking; and the staffs at VisitPhilly.com, Historic Philadelphia,
The National Park Service, the Barnes Foundation, the Philadelphia Museum
of Art, The Franklin Institute, The Museum of the American Revolution,
the National Constitution Center, and the Philadelphia Zoo for their help.

All the information in this guidebook is subject to change.
We recommend that you call ahead to obtain current
information before traveling.

Globe Pequot

An imprint of The Rowman & Littlefield Publishing Group, Inc.
4501 Forbes Blvd., Ste. 200
Lanham, MD 20706
www.rowman.com

Distributed by NATIONAL BOOK NETWORK

Copyright © 2020 Eileen Ogintz

Cover images © iStock/Getty Images Plus/moonery

All rights reserved. No part of this book may be reproduced in any form or by any
electronic or mechanical means, including information storage and retrieval systems,
without written permission from the publisher, except by a reviewer who may quote
passages in a review.

British Library Cataloguing in Publication Information available

Library of Congress Cataloging-in-Publication Data available

ISBN 978-1-4930-4632-4 (paper : alk. paper)
ISBN 978-1-4930-4633-1 (electronic)

♾™ The paper used in this publication meets the minimum requirements of
American National Standard for Information Sciences—Permanence of Paper for
Printed Library Materials, ANSI/NISO Z39.48-1992

CONTENTS

D0485757

1
Welcome to the City of Brotherly Love!

Have your time machine?

Philadelphia is the place in which you can travel to the past to experience the Revolutionary Days, when Thomas Jefferson, Betsy Ross, George Washington, and Ben Franklin were here—walking some of the same streets you are!

This is the city where Thomas Jefferson wrote the Declaration of Independence, where The Constitution was written and signed, and where Betsy Ross created the first American Flag. Philadelphia is home to the Liberty Bell, as famous for its big crack as it is for being a symbol of American independence. You will want to visit all of the historic sites—more about those in the next chapters.

DID YOU KNOW?

One of Philadelphia's best-known landmarks is the **LOVE statue**—the Robert Indiana sculpture in John F. Kennedy Plaza (or LOVE Park, as many now call it; North 15th Street and Arch Street). A mini sculpture always makes a good souvenir or a t-shirt that says XOXO. You can buy them at the **Independence Visitor Center** (599 Market St., 1 N. Independence Mall W.; 800-537-7676; phlvisitorcenter.com) gift shop.

{ WHAT'S COOL? Taking a cruise from Philadelphia (philadelphiacruiseguide.com). Several cruise lines now sail from Philadelphia to Bermuda, the Caribbean, and Canada.

But there is so much to do here no matter what you like—science and art museums; sports teams for every season, music and theater, festivals, and plenty of places for fun outside, even a Philly-themed mini golf course at Franklin Square and roller skating and ice skating at the Delaware River Waterfront (121 N. Columbus Blvd.; 215-922-2FUN; delawareriverwaterfront.com). Fairmount Park (Reservoir Drive; visitphilly.com/things-to-do/attractions/fairmount-park) is the biggest city park in the country!

Philadelphia is also known for its famous neighborhoods with names like Society Hill, Rittenhouse Square, East Passyunk, and Fishtown.

- **Chinatown** is packed with restaurants and stores that represent Asia, **Society Hill** is famous for its Colonial homes and winding cobblestone streets, and **South Philly** is home to the city's stadiums.

- **Center City**—the core of downtown Philadelphia— is the most well-known and includes historic **Rittenhouse Square** with its distinctive historic houses. Center City is easy to navigate. Thanks to William Penn's layout, Center City is on a grid, with numbered streets running north and south and named streets (mostly tree names) running east and west.

- **Old City** is next to **Independence Mall** and the **Liberty Bell Center** (526 Market St.) and still has cobblestones streets. Historic Rittenhouse Square was one of the first squares planned by William Penn in the 17th century. It is popular with visitors for its restaurants, shops, festivals, and of course the kid-friendly park in the middle where you can have a picnic or race around the circular walk.

{ WHAT'S COOL? The public art at Rittenhouse Square, including the **Duck Girl of 1911**—a sculpture of a girl carrying a duck in the reflecting pool, and **Billy**, a 2-foot-high bronze Billy goat. There's also a sculpture of two children holding up a sundial with a giant sunflower head. In the flower bed between the sundial and central plaza, there's the **Giant Frog** made from granite, and two small stone dogs.

A LOCAL KID SAYS:
Kids should come to the Barnes to see all the artwork. There is so much in just one room! I really liked seeing Monet paintings at the Barnes because I studied them in school.
—Valerie, 13, Philadelphia

DID YOU KNOW?

Philadelphia was declared the first capital of the US in 1790.

Philadelphia is the fifth largest city in the US.

- **Germantown** is one of the oldest city neighborhoods, and today the place to see local artists' work is at the **iMPeRFeCT Gallery** (5539 Germantown Ave.; imperfectgallery.squarespace.com). Also visit **Cliveden** (6401 Germantown Ave.; 215-848-1777; cliveden.org), where the only battle within Philadelphia was fought during the American Revolution.

- You'll find the city's famous museums, including The Franklin Institute (222 N. 20th St.; 215-448-1200; fi.edu), the Barnes Foundation (2025 Benjamin Franklin Pkwy.; 215-278-7000; barnesfoundation.org), and more, along the Benjamin Franklin Parkway in Logan Square, as well as City Hall (1400 John F. Kennedy Blvd.), which people say is an architectural wedding cake with all kinds of carvings. The famous LOVE statue and park are also near here. And if you are visiting during a holiday, this is where you'll see the Thanksgiving Day Parade and July Fourth festivities.

- Philadelphia also is a great place to try some new foods. Have you ever had a cheesesteak sandwich? It's a must!

{ WHAT'S COOL? All the art! Philadelphia is considered the mural capital of the country, with more than 2,000 outdoor wall murals!

How Philadelphia Got Its Name— and Nicknames

In Greek, Philadelphia means "brotherly love." The city was founded and named by William Penn in 1682. He wanted it to be a place where everyone could worship freely. That's why Philadelphia became the first city in the New World to guarantee religious freedom.

Today, Philadelphia has many nicknames, including Philly, The City of Brotherly Love, The Birthplace of America, The City that Loves You Back, The City of Neighborhoods, The Quaker City, and The Cradle of Liberty. What's your favorite?

DID YOU KNOW?

The massive bronze statue of William Penn atop the clock tower at City Hall is 37 feet tall and weighs 27 tons. You can stand at William Penn's feet when you visit City Hall's observation deck.

Philadelphia Firsts

Count them! Philadelphia has bragging rights to being first in lots of things, including these nine:

- The world's first computer was developed at the University of Pennsylvania. Named ENIAC, it was 150 feet wide!

- The first hospital and children's hospital in the country.

- The first Thanksgiving Day Parade in 1920.

- The first professional football game—when The Philadelphia Eagles beat the Cincinnati Reds at Temple Stadium on November 7, 1934.

- The First US Mint opened in 1792. At least half the coins in the country are made here. Check for the trademark "P" that means they were made in Philadelphia.

- The first zoo in the country, The Philadelphia Zoo, opened in 1874.

- The nation's first library was founded here by Benjamin Franklin in 1731.

- The first daily newspaper, *The Philadelphia Packet and Daily Advertiser,* was founded in 1784; *The Philadelphia Tribune,* founded a hundred years later, is the oldest continuously published African American newspaper.

- The first African American Church, Mother Bethel A.M.E Church was established in 1794. It served an important role in the Underground Railroad, providing shelter to escaped slaves on the run.

DID YOU KNOW?

Philadelphians were protesting against slavery more than 100 years before the Civil War. The first anti-slavery protest in the country was held here in 1688.

TELL THE ADULTS

Purchasing a **Philadelphia CityPASS** (citypass. com/Philadelphia) will save you nearly half the cost of admission if you plan to visit at least three of the city's major attractions, including the Philly Trolley Works Tour, the Liberty Observation Deck, the Philadelphia Zoo, Museum of the American Revolution, and The Franklin Institute. The pass also saves time and allows you to skip lines!

However, Philadelphia has a lot more to offer than historic sites and museums! Leave plenty of time to explore the city's neighborhoods. Join **Philly Friends** (visitphilly.com), locals who are glad to share their city with visitors.

Make sure everyone has a say in where you are going and what you are doing. The Hop-on Hop-Off Philadelphia City Sightseeing tours can help you get your bearings.

The PhillyFunGuide.com has discounted offers for entertainment events every week.

Time Out Philadelphia lists current family events at timeout.com/philadelphia/things-to-do/best -things-to-do-in-philadelphia-with-kids; MetroKids (metrokids.com) provides fun events in Philadelphia, South Jersey, and Delaware.

WELCOME TO PHILADELPHIA

Fill in the missing letters to spell out the mystery words.
(You will need to use some of the secret letters twice!)

Benjamin Frank__in
(7)

Elfret__'s Alley
(5)

L__gan Square
(3)

The Philadelphia __ribune
(4)

William P__nn
(6)

Delaware Ri__er Waterfront
(9)

Fai__mount Park
(2)

Center Cit__
(8)

__etsy Ross
(1)

{ **WHAT'S COOL?** A tree that went to the moon and back is growing in Washington Square.

___ ___ ___ ___ ___ ___ ___ ___ ___   ___ ___ ___ ___
(1) (2) (3) (4) (5) (6) (2) (7) (8)   (7) (3) (9) (6)

See page 133 for the answer!

2

The Most Famous
Philadelphian

Benjamin Franklin's father

wanted him to become a candle and soap maker when he grew up. But Benjamin Franklin had other plans! He had wanted to go to sea and threatened to run away if his dad made him join the family business.

Instead, his dad came up with another idea. When Franklin was 12, he was sent to work with his older brother as an apprentice, to learn his printing business. Franklin didn't last there either—he thought his brother was too strict so he ran away, setting up his own printing business.

That was only the beginning of course. Franklin—who had only two years of formal schooling—famously became one of our country's Founding Fathers. But he was much more than a politician. He was a scientist and an environmentalist, a diplomat who served in Paris, a successful businessman, newspaper founder, and an inventor.

DID YOU KNOW?

The Founding Fathers were the politicians and writers who led the American Revolution. They included four future presidents—George Washington, James Madison, Thomas Jefferson, and John Adams.

WHAT'S COOL? Watching park rangers demonstrate printing—18th-century style—at the **Franklin Court Printing Office** in the **Independence National Historical Park** (143 S. 3rd St.; 215-965-2305; nps.gov/inde/planyourvisit/printingoffice.htm). There were no computers in Benjamin Franklin's day. Books, newspapers, and even paper money were printed on a printing press. Printers spelled out everything with lead letters, putting them in one block at a time, upside down. Pictures were made by carving images into a block of wood. Printers inked the lead type and wood cuts, and then pressed them against paper, printing one sheet at a time.

Did you know Benjamin Franklin invented swim fins when he was only 11? Centuries before windsurfing, Franklin discovered he could harness the power of the wind with his kite and be pulled effortlessly across a mile-wide pond.

He discovered new ways to generate, store, and deploy electricity and even coined the term *battery*. He tried hard to improve everyone's life, from organizing the first public library and public hospital, to starting one of the country's first volunteer fire departments, to shaping the future of the US postal system.

Not only was he really smart, but people really liked him. He made friends wherever he went and over his lifetime, wrote them thousands of letters—no small task when you are as busy as he was! He got to know scientists in fields today known as physics, chemistry, biology, botany, and paleontology. Franklin proposed the creation of the American Philosophical Society (104 and 105 S. 5th St.; 215-440-3400; amphilsoc.org), an organization to share and exchange knowledge. The headquarters was set up in Philadelphia, where it remains to this day. Thanks to Franklin, the American Philosophical Society became a world-renowned institution.

While living in London, Franklin participated in a seed exchange with a network of scientists. His wife, Deborah, often acted as an intermediary from their home in Franklin Court, passing along seeds to Franklin's friends and planting some in their garden in Philadelphia.

Are you dutiful? Ambitious? Rebellious? Motivated to improve? Persuasive?

A LOCAL KID SAYS:
My favorite person from revolutionary times was Abigail Adams because she showed how women could do the same things as men.
—Charlotte, 9

DID YOU KNOW?

Alexander Hamilton was another important Founding Father. He helped shape American finance and the Constitution, and he was also a media tycoon who founded *The New York Post*. However, he might be best remembered for getting killed in a duel. Lin-Manuel Miranda's 2015 Broadway musical, *Hamilton*, introduced the Founding Father's life and legacy to a whole new generation.

Benjamin Franklin was all of those things. And his ideas still influence the way we live today.

You can see what traits you share with Franklin at the Benjamin Franklin Museum (Franklin Court, 317 Chestnut St.; 267-514-1522; nps.gov/inde/planyourvisit/benjamin franklinmuseum.htm), where each room focuses on a particular trait with interactive exhibits and touch screens. An additional area called the Library presents a video with excerpts from Franklin's autobiography.

Do you have a favorite personality trait?

WHAT'S COOL? Trying Ben Franklin's favorite invention at the Benjamin Franklin Museum—the **Virtual Glass Armonica**. You can play music with specially designed glass bowls.

The Most Famous Flag—and Flag Maker

Betsy Ross wasn't famous in her lifetime for making the first American flag.

In fact, it was no great honor to be chosen for the job. George Washington and two other members of the Flag Committee asked her because she was in the upholstery business and knew how to do the job.

Ross was newly widowed and struggling to keep her upholstery business going when the Flag Committee came to her house and showed her a design for a flag. Until then, each of the colonies had used different flags.

Originally, they wanted the stars to have six points, but she convinced them five-pointed stars would be a lot quicker to sew.

Betsy Ross finished the flag either in late May or early June 1776. It wasn't until nearly a year later, though, that the Continental Congress, seeking to promote national

{ WHAT'S COOL? Solving a "history mystery" at the Betsy Ross House. All you need is the kid's audio guide!

pride and unity, adopted the national flag with its 13 stars—one for each of the original colonies. Ross continued to make flags, later working with her daughter Clarissa and providing hundreds of flags to the government.

You can ask her about it yourself at the **Betsy Ross House** (239 Arch St.; 215-686-1252; historicphiladelphia.org/betsy-ross-house). You can see her work and learn what life was like in 18th-century Philadelphia.

Philis, a freed African American woman, will be there too and can tell you what life was like for her community in Philadelphia in those days.

Ready to raise the flag? Join Betsy on summer days at 10 a.m.!

DID YOU KNOW?

Betsy Ross made flags for more than 50 years with her daughter Clarissa's help.

TELL THE ADULTS

There are lots of places in Philadelphia for "living history" interactions and experiences, especially during the summer months. Here are a few:

- The **Once Upon a Nation Storytelling Benches** (historicphiladelphia.org/once-upon-a-nation/storytelling-benches) in Historic Philadelphia—visit all 13 and get a free Parx Liberty Carousel ride in Franklin Square.

- Listen to **History Makers** as they read from the Declaration of Independence many days over the summer (historicphiladelphia.org/once-upon-a-nation/historical-performances).

DID YOU KNOW?

You may see visitors toss pennies onto Benjamin Franklin's grave at **Christ Church Burial Grounds** (20 N. American St., on 2nd, above Market Street; 215-922-1695; christchurchphila.org) because he famously said, "A penny saved is a penny earned." BUT DON'T DO IT—the discarded coins damage the grave marker.

WHAT'S COOL? The free app that includes the **In Franklin's Footsteps** audio tour. Search "NPS Independence" on the App Store or Google Play to download.

- Meet citizens of 18th- and 19th-century Philadelphia at **Independence Visitor Center** (599 Market St., 1 N. Independence Mall West; 800-537-7676; phlvisitorcenter.com) and **Carpenter's Hall** (carpentershall.org) and hear firsthand what it was like to live in Colonial times. Pick up a *Historic Philadelphia Gazette* for a daily schedule.

- In summer, see how weapons were built for the Revolutionary Army at **Hopewell Furnace National Historic Site** (2 Mark Bird Ln., Elverson, PA; 610-582-8773; nps.gov/hofu/index.htm), about an hour's drive outside of Philadelphia, where cannons, shots, and shells were made.

- Also in summer, you can join the Continental Army at the **Military Muster** that takes place at the Signers' Garden at the corner of 5th and Chestnut Streets, across the street from Independence Hall.

Mini Golf, Chinese Lanterns & More

What do you want to do first?

Play mini-golf on a Philly-themed course—each hole is designed after favorite Philly spots like the Liberty Bell—or ride the **Parx Liberty Carousel**? Maybe play on the playground or grab a burger and shake at **SquareBurger**. You can do that and more at **Franklin Square** (200 N. 6th St.; historicphiladelphia.org/franklin-square/what-to-see) in the heart of Historic Philadelphia. It's one of the 5 original open-space parks planned by William Penn when he laid out the city of Philadelphia in 1682.

Today, it's family-central in Center City, thanks to Historic Philadelphia (historicphiladelphia.org) with Easter scavenger hunts and Christmas festivities. The **Philadelphia Chinese Lantern Festival** lights up **Franklin Square** throughout May and June with 20,000 LED lights and special performances, and the Franklin Square Fountain water, light and music show debuts on July 31, with timed performances during the day and night.

Take a few minutes at the **Living Flame Memorial**, dedicated to Philadelphia's fallen police officers and firefighters.

SECRET CODE

Have you ever created a secret code with your friends?
See if you can figure out what famous phrase Benjamin
Franklin said using the code below.

A=X	E=V	I=T	M=L	Q=J	U=H	Y=A
B=Y	F=W	J=O	N=M	R=K	V=C	Z=B
C=Z	G=R	K=P	O=N	S=F	W=D	
D=U	H=S	L=Q	P=I	T=G	X=E	

"Y IGDX SGPXOW PH IUX ZXHI KJHHXHHPJO."

" __ _____ _____

__ ___ ____

_____ "

See page 134 for the answer!

DID YOU KNOW?

Ben Franklin gave away pet
squirrels known as "skuggs."

3

The Country's Most
Historic Square Mile

There was no air conditioning,

and it was really hot that summer of 1776.

Many of the 56 delegates who had gathered at the Pennsylvania State House were far from home and could only keep in touch with their families through letters. There was no email or texting of course.

The Second Continental Congress had begun meeting the year before. The delegates established a Continental Army and elected George Washington as commander in chief, but they were still hoping for a peaceful resolution with King George III. He wouldn't hear their petition.

WHAT'S COOL? Posing like **The Signer** statue for a photo. **The Signer** commemorates the spirit and deeds of all those who devoted their lives to the cause of American freedom.

DID YOU KNOW?

The first time the formal term "The United States of America" was used was in the Declaration of Independence.

So, on June 7, 1776, Virginia delegate Richard Henry Lee put forward the resolution for independence. Voting was postponed to get more of the delegates to agree. A committee of five delegates was assigned to draft a document of independence: John Adams (MA), Benjamin Franklin (PA), Thomas Jefferson (VA), Roger Sherman (CT), and Robert R. Livingston (NY). Think of it like a group project you might do at school.

Jefferson wrote most of it in a little more than two weeks in the house where he was staying at 7th and Market Street. "We hold these truths to be self-evident, that all men are created equal, that they are endowed . . . with certain unalienable rights, that among these are Life, Liberty, and the Pursuit of Happiness."

A LOCAL KID SAYS:
A good Philadelphia souvenir is a mini copy of the Declaration of Independence.
—Lilly, 10

But women and African Americans were left out. Do you think that was fair? They certainly didn't!

The Declaration of Independence lists all the grievances the colonists had against King George for taking away their rights as English citizens. Since the King was "unfit to be the ruler of a free People," they said, they were declaring that the 13 colonies were now "free and independent states."

On July 2, 1776, the delegates to the Second Continental Congress voted for independence, but they continued to argue about every word, making 86 changes to the committee's draft. How do you think Jefferson felt? Everyone had to make compromises.

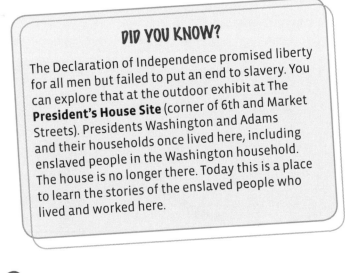

DID YOU KNOW?

The Declaration of Independence promised liberty for all men but failed to put an end to slavery. You can explore that at the outdoor exhibit at The **President's House Site** (corner of 6th and Market Streets). Presidents Washington and Adams and their households once lived here, including enslaved people in the Washington household. The house is no longer there. Today this is a place to learn the stories of the enslaved people who lived and worked here.

None of Jefferson's original drafts have survived, but the rough draft he shared with Benjamin Franklin and John Adams survives in the Library of Congress. Check out their handwritten edits at loc.gov/exhibits/declara/images/draft1.jpg.

See where the delegates argued and ultimately signed the Declaration of Independence and the US Constitution in the Assembly Room of Independence Hall.

On July 4, Congress voted again, and this time they approved the wording. But 50 of the delegates didn't actually sign it for another month, and the last 6 over the next 18 months. (It may have been even longer, as some historians speculate that Thomas McKean didn't pen his name until 1781.)

{ WHAT'S COOL? The odd way some letters look in historic documents—like the long "s" that looks like a lowercase "f" stuck in the wrong spot.

signature

The Constitution wasn't written and finalized until September 17, 1787, 11 years later, and it took another year before the new government began to operate under the Constitution. James Madison wrote the document that formed the basis of the Constitution.

You can see surviving copies of the Declaration of Independence, the Articles of Confederation, and the Constitution along with the silver inkstand that, according to tradition, was used during the signing of the Declaration and Constitution in the Great Essentials Exhibit in the West Wing of Independence Hall.

The original US Constitution has 4,543 words, including the signatures. Today it has 7,591 words, including the 27 amendments added over 200 years. It is the oldest and shortest-written Constitution of any major government in the world.

When the Constitution was signed, the US population was 4 million. It is now more than 327 million. But the Constitution is still the basis of our government.

Pretty amazing!

{ **WHAT'S COOL?** Touring Thomas Jefferson's former house, **The Declaration House** (4 S. 7th St.; 800-537-7676; phlvisitorcenter.com/things-to-do/declaration-house), a few blocks from Independence Hall. Several rooms in the house have been restored to appear as they did when Jefferson lived there and wrote the Declaration of Independence.

The Liberty Bell

At first, no one considered the Pennsylvania State House bell any kind of symbol. It simply rang in the tower of the Pennsylvania State House to call lawmakers to their meetings and the townspeople together to hear the reading of the news.

It wasn't even a symbol of liberty during the Revolutionary War—that didn't happen until the 1830s. The inscription "Proclaim Liberty Throughout All the Land Unto All the Inhabitants Thereof" became the rallying cry, first for the anti-slavery movement, and later for those fighting for women's rights.

The first bell, ordered in 1751 from England, cracked on the first test ring. It was melted down and a new one was made in Philadelphia. No one knows exactly when that one cracked— sometime in the mid-19th century. Look closely and you can see the drill bit marks where metal workers attempted but failed to fix the crack.

That didn't really matter. By the late 1800s, the Liberty Bell was so famous that it was exhibited across the country. Today, it is an international symbol of liberty.

No one living today has heard the bell ring freely.

DID YOU KNOW?

The Liberty Bell isn't the only bell in Independence Park. The **Centennial Bell**, made for the nation's 100th birthday, still rings every hour in the tower of Independence Hall. The Bicentennial Bell was given to the people of the US by Great Britain in 1976.

31

TELL THE ADULTS

The **Junior Ranger Challenge** app for iPhone
and iPad gives kids an opportunity to learn about
Independence National Historical Park (143 S. 3rd
St.; 215-965-2305; nps.gov/inde/learn/kidsyouth/
beajuniorranger.htm) before they arrive. If apps
aren't your thing, kids can also pick up Junior Ranger
Activity Booklets when they arrive.

Start at the **Independence Visitor Center**
(599 Market St., 1 N. Independence Mall West;
800-537-7676; phlvisitorcenter.com). There is no fee
to enter the building but you will need timed entry
Independence Hall tickets. They are distributed each
day (March through December) from the Ranger's
Desk in the Independence Visitor Center. For the
best selection of times, arrive early. For advance
ticket reservations
(handling fee applies),
call (877) 444-6777 or
log on to recreation.gov.

DID YOU KNOW?

In 1777, Philadelphia was
the nation's largest city with
40,000 residents—smaller
than many suburbs today.

DID YOU KNOW?

John Hancock was the first to sign the Declaration of Independence. Maybe that's why he signed his name so large. All of the signers risked their lives when they signed because the King of England considered them to be traitors.

Check out this link for more information about obtaining Independence Hall tickets: nps.gov/inde/planyourvisit/independencehalltickets.htm.

No tickets are needed at the Liberty Bell; admission is free and entrance is first-come, first-served.

Park Rangers suggest carrying as small a bag as possible since you will need to pass through security.

WHAT'S COOL? Becoming a junior ranger at Independence National Historical Park (143 S. 3rd St.; 215-965-2305; nps.gov/inde). Earn trading cards by answering questions from the National Park Rangers!

National Constitution Center

It may be the greatest vision of human freedom, but more than 200 years later Americans continue to debate what the framers of the Constitution intended.

The interactive **National Constitution Center** (Independence Mall, 525 Arch St.; 215-409-6700; constitution center.org) can help you understand why the US Constitution is as important today as it was when it was drafted. See some rare handwritten drafts of the document and take time to see the *Freedom Rising* multimedia production that tells the story of the Constitution. The center's main exhibit, *The Story of We the People,* includes interactive exhibits. In Signers' Hall you can walk among the 42 life-size bronze statues of those who participated in the signing of the Constitution on September 17, 1787.

There are also archeological artifacts uncovered near here that will give you a glimpse into what life was like in the 1700s. The *Civil War and Reconstruction* exhibit explores how the nation transformed the Constitution after the Civil War to more fully embrace the Declaration of Independence's promise of liberty and equality.

The museum isn't only about history. There are *Living News* performances in which today's headlines become performances with video and music with actors who play multiple roles.

PHILADELPHIA WORD SCRAMBLE

Since Philadelphia was the seat of the Second Continental Congress, it's a place where lots of important people met and made decisions. Unscramble some of the famous names below!

ENIBMANJ IARNKLFN

___ ___ ___ ___ ___ ___ ___ ___   ___ ___ ___ ___ ___ ___ ___ ___

GREOR SNRMEHA

___ ___ ___ ___ ___   ___ ___ ___ ___ ___ ___ ___

HOTAMS EROJNSEFF

___ ___ ___ ___ ___ ___   ___ ___ ___ ___ ___ ___ ___ ___ ___

JNHO MASDA

___ ___ ___ ___   ___ ___ ___ ___ ___

EGORGE WTHIANGSON

___ ___ ___ ___ ___ ___   ___ ___ ___ ___ ___ ___ ___ ___ ___ ___

HNOJ HCANCOK

___ ___ ___ ___   ___ ___ ___ ___ ___ ___ ___

See page 134 for the answers!

DID YOU KNOW?

The oldest person to sign the Constitution was Benjamin Franklin, then 81. The youngest was Jonathan Dayton, 26, of New Jersey.

4
Join the American Revolution!

Do you like history?

If you do, you're going to love the Museum of the American Revolution (101 S. 3rd St.; 215-253-6731; amrevmuseum.org).

First, there is so much cool stuff to see—everything from Revolutionary War weapons to soldiers' letters and a soldier's wooden canteen to drinking cups with political slogans—they didn't have reusable water bottles in those days!

Check out the baby booties made from the coat of a British foot soldier and the pair of 18th-century slave shackles meant for a child.

But this isn't just a place to look at things. You can join the angry mob that pulls down a statue of King George III. Face the enemy in battle. And think about whether you would have been loyal to the king, even if you thought he wasn't treating the colonists well, or whether you would have risked everything to fight for independence.

{ WHAT'S COOL? The interactive exhibits at the **National Museum of American Jewish History** (101 S. Independence Mall East; 215-923-3811; nmajh.org)—you'll find everything from a covered wagon to an antique assembly line.

At the replica of Boston's Liberty Tree, think about which side you would have been on—this is where the colonists first debated whether to revolt against the king.

At the Battlefield Theater, you'll feel what it was like to be on the Continental Army's front line. There's a re-creation of Independence Hall that was a prison for American soldiers during the British occupation of Philadelphia.

You'll also see George Washington's war tent as part of a multimedia show about his leadership. And at the Legacy Theater, you're invited to think about how liberty and equality are still so important.

DID YOU KNOW?

You can see the original tent that George Washington used as his command center at the **Museum of the American Revolution**.

At the museum, you can also see the important role women, African Americans, and Native Americans played in the war effort. Learn about Elizabeth "Mumbet" Freeman, an enslaved woman who sued for her freedom and won; Deborah Sampson, who dressed as a man to fight in the Continental Army; Phillis Wheatley, America's first published black female poet; and Two Kettles Together, a Native American woman who fought in the Battle of Oriskany alongside her husband.

The museum offers special interactive events on many holidays. You might be able to make a flag or see how shoes were made for the army—by hand!

In the museum's discovery center, Revolution Place, the whole family can explore 18th-century Philadelphia

DID YOU KNOW?

When the American troops ran low on supplies, a man named Haym Salomon helped pay for the war—so much so that he died penniless. He is buried at **Congregation Mikveh Israel Cemetery** (825 Spruce St.; mikvehisrael.org).

WHAT'S COOL? The **Podcast Through History** series about Valley Forge—the Continental Army's winter encampment in 1777 to 1778—tells the story through the eyes of those who were there, including General Washington. It's on YouTube. You can visit **Valley Forge National Historic Park** (1400 N. Outer Line Dr., King of Prussia, PA; 610-783-1000; nps.gov/vafo) the site where the tired, cold, and inadequately equipped troops were transformed into a great fighting force.

through immersive environments, interactive touchscreens, reproduction objects, and special programs.

You can join the Continental Army thanks to a digital touchscreen. Sign your name on the enlistment form using a quill pen and then climb inside a recreated soldier's tent. It was pretty small! Did anyone in your family serve in the Continental Army? You can search to see if anyone with your family's name did.

At the re-created Three Tun Tavern—the real one was located across the street from the museum—you can put objects such as a tea cup, a twist of tobacco, and a man's wallet on the digital tabletops and see who might have used them and where they were made. During the Revolutionary era, people received their news from newspapers and by word of mouth at taverns where they ate food and talked about issues.

If you're wondering what family life was like in those days, you can visit an 18th-century parlor—kind of like a family room. Use the digital touchscreens to learn about the families who lived nearby.

41

Washington's Christmas Crossing

You know the famous painting—General George Washington and more than 2,000 of his troops crossing the Delaware River on Christmas night 1776 in a terrible winter storm. It was painted by Emanuel Leutze in 1851 and is in the Metropolitan Museum of Art in New York City.

Over the years, Washington's crossing became one of the most remembered moments of the Revolutionary War. The soldiers were cold and tired. Morale was low. Many wanted to go home. Washington gave one of his most famous speeches to convince the troops to stay at least until after the battle.

Early the next morning, after they crossed the river, Washington and his troops surprised the Hessian mercenary soldiers fighting for the British at Trenton, New Jersey. Most of them

DID YOU KNOW?

The construction of the Museum of the American Revolution unearthed many historic items from Colonial times. See some of the things people threw in the historic outhouse that was part of the archeological excavation—they used it as a trash can in those days.

were asleep. The Battle of Trenton ended quickly, was a huge victory for Washington, and turned the tide of the war.

You can visit the **Washington Crossing Historic Park** (1112 River Rd., Washington Crossing, PA; 215-493-4076; washingtoncrossing park.org) in Bucks County outside of Philadelphia on the Pennsylvania side where Washington and his troops crossed. See the Thompson-Neely House that served as a hospital for the injured that winter. Some of the soldiers who died are buried here. Check out the historic grist mill. There's also the McConkey Ferry Inn where Washington and his aides planned the Delaware River crossing. You can see the replicas of the boats they used.

Climb to the top of Bowman's Hill Tower—125 feet up— for a great view! The best part: There's lots of room to run around and play.

You also may want to visit **Valley Forge National Historical Park** (1400 N. Outer Line Dr., King of Prussia, PA; 610-783-1000; nps.gov/vafo)—this was the site of the 1777 to 1778 winter encampment and where, under great sacrifice, the Continental Army became a great fighting force.

Your Freedom or
Your Country's Freedom

James Forten was just 14 when he signed up to help the Patriots, joining the crew of a ship hunting for British warships.

He was a free young black man living in Philadelphia and thought independence from Britain would help African Americans live better lives.

Enslaved blacks had a much harder choice to make because the British were offering freedom to enslaved men who signed up, and thousands did.

Eventually many states recruited slaves for military service, usually in exchange for their freedom. By the end of the war, some 9,000 African Americans had served the American cause as soldiers, sailors, spies, servants, and even drummers.

African Americans who lived in Philadelphia between 1776 and 1876 also fought for independence, first from Great Britain and later from slavery. In Philadelphia, they used newspapers, including *The Liberator, The Freeman,* and the *North Star* to voice their opinions and create positive change. They helped escaped slaves navigate the Underground Railroad.

Forten was taken prisoner by the British, but he survived the war and became a successful Philadelphia businessman.

Meet more African American Philadelphians who made a difference at the **African American Museum** (701 Arch St.; 215-574-0380; aampmuseum.org) in Historic Philadelphia. The Children's Corner explores what it was like to be a kid in Philadelphia from 1779 through 1876. Come for a special family workshop the second Saturday of every month!

A LOCAL KID SAYS:
The evolution of the flag was my favorite exhibit at the Museum of the American Revolution. Kids don't realize that people come from all over to see Philadelphia's history from that time!
—Zack, 14

There are many places in and outside of Philadelphia to explore more Revolutionary War history, including these that kids will like:

- **Fort Mifflin** (1 Fort Mifflin Rd.; 215-685-4167; fortmifflin.us), where 400 soldiers survived the cold for six weeks in 1777 to fend off British ships trying to bring supplies to British-occupied Philadelphia. You can tour the barracks, see the blacksmith shop, view a cannon demonstration, and more.

- **Peter Wentz Farmstead** (2030 Shearer Rd., Lansdale, PA; 610-584-5104; peterwentz farmsteadsociety.org) served as General Washington's temporary headquarters in October 1777 as he planned what ultimately would be a major defeat for the Revolutionary Army at Germantown. See livestock, kitchens, and 1777-inspired recreations of farm life.

- **Valley Forge National Historical Park** (1400 N. Outer Line Dr., King of Prussia, PA; 610-783-1000; nps.gov/vafo), the site of the 1777 to 1778 winter encampment of George Washington's

Continental Army. This is a great place to hike—there are 26 miles of trails! There are also tours, exhibits, live demonstrations, children's activities, and more.

- **Christ Church and Burial Grounds** (20 N. American St.; 215-922-1695; christchurchphila .org). This church was where 15 signers of the Declaration of Independence worshipped. The church is still active today and is called "America's Church." Come for services or take a self-guided or guided tour offered daily. The church's cemetery dates from 1719 and besides the graves of Benjamin and Deborah Franklin, you can find those of others who fought for independence. The cemetery offers self-guided and guided tours daily for a small fee.

DID YOU KNOW?

Polish war hero Thaddeus Kosciuszko helped the Continental Army beat the Redcoats in several battles. You can learn more about his contributions—he was an engineering genius—at the **Polish American Cultural Center** (308 Walnut St.; 215-922-1700; polishamericancenter.org/history.htm).

WHAT'S COOL? Eating at **City Tavern** (138 S. 2nd St. at Walnut St.; 215-413-1443; citytavern.com) where George Washington, Thomas Jefferson, and Ben Franklin, among others, gathered for happy hour. You can eat here today!

CROSSING THE DELAWARE

Help General George Washington find his way across the Delaware River in the dark. Be careful not to wake the British soldiers and ruin the surprise!

See page 134 for the answer!

5

Cheesesteak, Pretzels, 13-Star Flags & More

When you are away from home,

it's always fun to try local brands and visit local restaurants.

Philadelphia is a great place to try new foods, especially when everyone in the family can sample something different!

Reading Terminal Market (51 N. 12th St.; 215-922-2317; readingterminalmarket.org) is a great place to do that any time of day. But first, look around the building! It's a National Historic Landmark that has been in the same place since 1893. When the Philadelphia and Reading Railroad Company bought the block for a new

terminal, the merchants already there didn't want to move, so the huge market was put beneath the train shed and tracks.

In those days there were nearly 800 spaces for merchants! Women could call in their orders and have them put on a commuter train for them to pick up. But by the 1970s, there were hardly any merchants left.

DID YOU KNOW?

Reading Terminal Market is the country's oldest continuously operating farmer's market. Back in the day, boys called "market brats" carried small orders to in-town customers.

Markets have been a part of Philadelphia since the city was first established—that's how Market Street first got its name when farmers, fisherman, and others started to sell their goods in one place. Today, Reading Terminal Market has more than eighty merchants and is a great place to see what is made locally and chat up local farmers and producers. Don't you like to know where your food comes from? That is how the Reading Terminal Market became successful again.

WHAT'S COOL? Trying local Philadelphia dishes for breakfast—like a Pork Roll (a bologna-like breakfast meat often served on a Kaiser roll with eggs and cheese) and Scrapple (a mixture of crispy fried pork, spices, and cornmeal).

You'll see fresh-baked Amish goods, produce direct from the field, unusual spices, free-range meats and poultry, flowers, ethnic foods, eggs and milk from local farms—as well as handmade crafts, jewelry, and clothes.

It will be hard to choose. Thai, Chinese, or sandwich? A hot dog, ribs, or a salad? Bassett's ice cream or a freshly baked cookie? Of course, you can have a cheesesteak! Take the chance to try something you haven't had before. There are plenty of options if you are vegetarian, vegan, or have food allergies, too.

Another good bet near a lot of the historic sites is The Bourse food hall (111 S. Independence Mall East; theboursephilly.com) at Independence Mall.

The Bourse was founded in 1891 by George Bortal and housed a stock exchange, maritime exchange, and

DID YOU KNOW?

The **Tasty Baking Company** (tastykake.com) revolutionized the snack cake industry with individually wrapped fruit pies more than 100 years ago. TastyKakes are still a go-to treat for Philadelphians.

WHAT'S COOL? A soft pretzel for breakfast! Get one at a bakery such as the **Philly Pretzel Factory** (phillypretzelfactory.com) or before noon at **Center City Pretzel Company** (centercitypretzel.com). Do what locals do—put mustard on pieces of pretzel.

grain-trading exchange all at the same time. Now the historic space is a popular food hall where you can get anything from ice cream to pancakes to tacos to grilled cheese to chai, to, of course, cheesesteak. Have you ever tried Filipino LALO—kabobs and rice? They are considered comfort food. Freebyrd Chicken offers fried chicken, and at Fry Café, you can get fries, chicken fingers, mac 'n' cheese, and more.

Philadelphia is famous for its neighborhoods and you will find plenty of good restaurants wherever you are. New ones are opening all the time!

If you're going to be outside of Philadelphia, you can check out how potato chips are made at Herr's Snack Factory (271 Old Baltimore Pike, Nottingham, PA; 800-637-6225; herrs.com/snackfactorytours.html) in Nottingham, Pennsylvania. It's a little more than an hour outside the city. If you can't get there, at least try Herr's chips with your sandwich.

What's your favorite Philadelphia meal?

Philly's Most Famous Sandwich

What kind of cheese do you want? Whiz? Provolone? American? And do you want onions?

That's all you need to know to order a cheesesteak, Philadelphia's most famous sandwich. Sorry vegetarians!

Pat Olivieri was a hot dog vendor when one day in 1930, he threw some beef from a butcher on the grill. A taxi driver asked for a steak sandwich. The story goes that by the next day, cabbies from around the city came demanding the delicious sandwich served up on a hoagie roll. Pretty soon

DID YOU KNOW?

Many locals prefer a roast pork sandwich to cheesesteak. Try one with broccoli rabe and provolone. Try one at **DiNic's** (tommydinics.com) in Reading Terminal Market. It has won awards!

Olivieri opened **Pat's King of Steaks** (1237 E. Passyunk Ave.; 215-468-1546; patskingofsteaks.com) and eventually cheese was added to the sandwich. Today you can still get cheesesteaks at Pat's 24 hours a day.

Geno's Steaks (1219 S. 9th St. and 9th and Passyunk Ave.; 215-389-0659; genosteaks.com) also is open 24/7 at its two locations.

You can get a cheesesteak at more than 50 places around Philadelphia, including **Campo's** (214 Market St.; 215-923-1000; camposdeli.com) just a few blocks from the Independence Visitor Center. It's been serving up cheesesteaks for more than 70 years.

Cheesesteaks are now so popular that there is even a **National Cheesesteak Day** (March 24) and a **Philly Cheesesteak and Food Fest** every fall. Check the events section of VisitPhilly.com for more information.

So, what's it going to be: with onions or without?

TELL THE ADULTS

Make Vacation a Food Adventure

You'll have plenty of options in Philadelphia. Encourage the kids to try new foods by ordering appetizer portions or sharing plates.

Here are options that VisitPhilly.com says families will love.

For breakfast, try **Marathon** (21 S. 16th St.; 215-569-3278 and 1818 Market St.; 215-561-1818, and 1839 Spruce St.; 215-731-0800; eatmarathon.com), which offers three casual restaurants conveniently placed throughout Center City that are perfect for early-riser breakfasts, as well as lunch and dinner. **Sabrina's Café & Spencer's Too** (1806 Callowhill St.; 215-636-9061; sabrinascafe.com) is also a good choice, but be aware it is so popular that there are sometimes lines out the door on weekends!

For ice cream, check out **The Franklin Fountain & Ice Cream Bar** (116 Market St.; 215-627-1899; franklinfountain.com). The historic district's Victorian ice cream saloon and nearby Art Deco–inspired walk-up bar combine forces on menus based on handmade ice cream, with splits, shakes, sundaes.

WHAT'S COOL? A visit to a fortune cookie company on a **Wok 'n Walk Tour** (josephpoon.com), that ends with a meal at a Chinatown restaurant.

For pizza, visit **Pizzeria Stella** (420 S. 2nd St.; 215-320-8000; pizzeriastella.net) just off South Street. On the menu: gourmet pizzas, pastas, salads, and house-made gelato made from a secret family recipe.

For comfort food, you can't go wrong at **Jones** (700 Chestnut St.; 215-223-5663; jones-restaurant .com). With its stylish setting right out of *The Brady Bunch*, this crowd-pleasing corner restaurant serves up classic comfort foods such as macaroni and cheese and meatloaf.

Spot Gourmet Burger (2821 W. Girard Ave.; 267-930-7370; spotburgers.com) is the place for burgers. Part of a food truck, this casual spot builds its burgers from beef, chicken, potatoes (and other veggies), and even serves its sirloin in 3-ounce sizes. Don't worry, there are fries, too.

For sushi, **POD** (3636 Sansom St.; 215-387-1803; podrestaurant.com) is the place. The setting is futuristic and the sushi arrives via conveyer belt.

Foodies won't want to miss **Chew Philly Food Tours** (215-600-4891; phillyfoodtours.com). This food tour is sprinkled with local history and a portion of ticket sales goes to Philadelphia non-profit The Food Trust.

For the health-conscious travelers in your group, **HipCityVeg** (121 S. Broad St.; 267-296-9001 and 214 S. 40th St.; 267-244-4342; hipcityveg.com) is a 100 percent plant-based, quick-casual cafe with several locations. Fans line up for indulgence-inspired crispy ranch "chick'n" sandwiches, Philly "steak," and green smoothies. There is also **P.S. & Co.** (1706 Locust St.; 215-985-1706; puresweets.com) for vegans and those on gluten-free diets.

WHAT'S COOL? A uniquely Philadelphia treat kids have loved for more than 130 years called **Goldenberg Peanut Chews** (peanutchews.com). They contain nuts, sweet syrup, and chocolate.

Souvenir Smarts

You'll find souvenirs everywhere you go in Philadelphia from street vendors to museums and neighborhood shops. A tee shirt or baseball cap ... a key chain ... a Benjamin Franklin magnet.

And don't forget outside of the city. **The King of Prussia Mall** (160 N. Gulph Rd., King of Prussia, PA; 610-265-5727; simon.com/mall/king-of-prussia) is the largest in the country with over 450 stores.

Inside the city, check out the kid-sized tricorn hats and 13-star flags at the **Betsy Ross House** (239 Arch St.; 215-686-1252; historicphiladelphia.org/betsy-ross-house); LOVE pencil sharpeners, key chains, kids' books, penny earrings, and more at the **Independence Visitor Center** (599 Market St., 1 N. Independence Mall West; 800-537-7676; phlvisitorcenter.com); $5 custom-made Philadelphia T shirts at **Old City T-Shirts and Souvenirs** (233 Church St.; 215-925-7860; oldcitytshirts.com); or a Chocolate Liberty Bell or LOVE statue at **Verde** (108 S. 13th St.; 215-546-8700; verdephiladelphia.com).

Whatever you think you want to buy, talk to your parents first about how much you can spend. Some families save loose change in a big jar for vacation souvenirs. That can really add up!

Think about buying something that will remind you of what you saw and did in Philadelphia. Resist impulse buys. Maybe you want to start a collection of Junior Ranger patches, stickers for your water bottle, or pins or key chains for your backpack.

A LOCAL KID SAYS:
Get something for a souvenir that says "I (heart) Philly."
—Rochelle, 10, Philadelphia

I ♥ PHILLY

WHAT DID YOU EAT TODAY?

Draw what you ate!

6

Sharks, Hippos, Gorillas,
Cheetahs & More

The animals are on the move!

Thanks to Zoo360, a Philadelphia Zoo (3400 W. Girard Ave.; philadelphiazoo.org)–wide network of see-through mesh trails, the animals can roam around above the zoo grounds like never before. It's the first such system in the country. And it means you can see the animals like never before—as you move, the animals in the zoo are moving with you!

There currently are six trails:

- Gorilla Treeway is 300-foot passageway 12 feet above you where the gorillas can explore among the trees.

- Treetop Trail is designed for monkeys and lemurs to travel from their habitats in the Rare Animal Conservation Center through the trees around Impala Plaza. You might also see black and white colobus monkeys, blue-eyed lemurs, and others here too.

- Great Ape Trail connects to the orangutan's outdoor yard, crossing 16 feet above you.

- Big Cat Crossing is a 330-foot mesh overhead passageway that extends from Big Cat Falls and the zoo's main path. Lions, tigers, pumas, and jaguars get to stretch their legs more than ever before!

A LOCAL KID SAYS:
Go play outside!
—Josiah, 10, Philadelphia

- **Meerkat Maze** is a winding path that includes lookouts. There is a maze alongside for kids to climb and play, just like the meerkats do.

- **Water Is Life** allows red pandas and giant otters to move about with overhead bridges, tunnels, and even a big slide. Don't miss the interactive water sculptures! See how each otter is unique—each with different white or cream fur on their throats and under their chins. When they meet, they rear up out of the water, as if to show another otter who they are!

Think about how the Philadelphia Zoo was America's first zoo and now is changing the way zoos are built. There is so much to see and do here it will be hard to decide where to go first. You'll definitely want to check out KidZooU, where you can get your hands dirty helping the animals at a wildlife workshop. You can also play next to the goats, explore the butterfly habitat, or watch ants move through their tunnels.

Do you want to see the zoo babies? Watch the spider monkeys swing 20 feet above you? Don't miss Tony the white rhino (he's the biggest animal at the zoo), and the giraffe family of Gus, Stella, Abigail, and Beau (they're the tallest).

WHAT'S COOL? Scratching a rhino's ear—with The Go Behind the Scenes meet-and-greet with your favorite animal at the Philadelphia Zoo.

At Penguin Point there is a colony of more than 20 Humboldt penguins. Their habitat is along the coast of Chile and Peru and they "co-parent." Before their babies are even born, each parent takes turns sitting on the egg while the other goes off to fish.

Maybe you want to see Bear Country, complete with waterfalls and brooks and bears from around the world.

In the summer, join the turtles, snakes, and lizards in the Reptile Exercise Yard basking in the sun. See animals you may never have met at the Rare Animal Conservation Center—monkeys with bright orange fur and bats with a 3-foot wingspan. This is the place to learn about the issues that impact their survival in the world.

Discover more than 100 birds, many of them endangered, at the McNeil Avian Center. If you're lucky, you might see a hornbill catch a bug right out of the air.

Take a selfie by jumping into the "pouch" of the giant kangaroo statue at the Outback Outpost.

What's your favorite animal?

DID YOU KNOW?

The Philadelphia Zoo was the first zoo in the US, opened in 1874. That's why it's called America's First Zoo. Today it is home to 1,300 animals, many of them endangered.

Sharks, Poisonous Frogs, Penguins & More

Ready to meet a Great Hammerhead shark?

You can do just that at **Adventure Aquarium** (1 Riverside Dr., Camden, NJ; 844-474-3474; adventureaquarium.com) just across the Delaware River from downtown Philadelphia in New Jersey. This shark got its name from the hammer shape of its head.

The aquarium has the only Great Hammerhead on exhibit in the country and the biggest collection of sharks on the East Coast—you'll see zebra sharks with their black stripes when they are young (they turn to spots when they are older), sand tigers sharks that look scarier than they are, silky sharks found all over the world in tropical waters, and nurse sharks that hang out in big groups—up to 40 of them! Ready to cross the Shark Bridge?

But the sharks are just some of the 8,500 animals here! Come face-to-face with turtles, stingrays, and all sorts of

creatures of the deep. You won't want to miss the cute African penguins (they are only about 2 feet tall and weigh just 8 pounds!). There's also Hippo Haven, where you can get nose-to-nose with the huge Nile hippos, Button and Jenny. They weigh 3,000 pounds each! You'll feel like you've been transported to an African river!

Check out Frog Alley in the KidZone, where frogs that look harmless are dangerous. When threatened, the Amazon milk frog produces a white poisonous substance and the poison dart frogs are also very toxic. There's also the Grotto touch tank with slimy warm-water creatures.

At Creature Feature, you can touch sea stars, anemones, sea cucumber, snails, and more.

Be prepared to get your hands wet!

DID YOU KNOW?

The **Philadelphia Zoo** (philadelphiazoo.org) donates thousands of dollars every year to support scientists and conservation projects around the globe, and you help it do that by paying admission, making donations, or becoming a member.

TELL THE ADULTS

Zoos and aquariums are great places for fun but also help kids understand why it is important to protect the environment. As you visit, talk to the kids about how your family can help the environment. Check to see if your membership at your local zoo or aquarium will get you in free!

Get a unique view of the animals at the zoo and sea creatures at the aquarium with overnight visits. **Adventure Aquarium** has the **Shark in the Dark Program** (aquaticsciences.org/education/deep_sleep .html), complete with a behind-the-scenes tour and an early morning experience with the African penguins and hippos.

Spend the Night at the Philadelphia Zoo (philadelphiazoo.org/Learn/Spend-the-Night-at-the-Zoo.htm) with animal keeper meet-and-greets, late night hikes, crafts, and more.

There are also **behind-the-scenes tours** (philadelphiazoo.org/Visit/Guided-Tours/Behind-the-Scenes.htm) at the Philadelphia Zoo and the chance for a **Meet Us in the Wild Field Program** (aquaticsciences.org/education/meet-us.html) at **Adventure Aquarium.**

And be sure the kids respect all fences, walls, and DO-NOT-ENTER signs. You don't want to be "that tourist."

If you have younger kids in the group, there's the **KidZone** at **Adventure Aquarium** and the **SEPTA PZ Express Kiddie Train**, the **Amazon Rainforest Carousel**, and **Swan Boats** at the Philadelphia Zoo.

Traveling Greener

The Philadelphia Zoo is focused on reducing its environmental footprint as well as helping protect endangered species. **KidZooU** (kidzoou.org) was designed to incorporate green elements such as geothermal walls and collecting rainwater to flush public toilets.

It's easy for you to travel greener:

- Use public transportation when possible.

- Tun off the lights and AC when you leave your hotel room or rental.

- Recycle!

- Reuse towels and take shorter showers.

- Use a reusable water bottle. Get stickers at the places you visit in Philadelphia to make it a special souvenir!

- Watch what you eat! Eat foods that are locally grown and raised, fished, or produced using sustainable practices.

WHAT'S COOL? The vertical farm at the Philadelphia Zoo's Urban Green area that produces food for the zoo's baby animals. You can hang out here, get lunch, and play.

CONNECT THE DOTS

Hammerhead sharks get their name from the unique shape of their heads, which allows them to see in many directions (up, down, left, and right) at the same time. This comes in handy when sharks are watching for signs of danger or looking for food. Hammerhead sharks eat just about anything—from squid, snakes, rays, and even other sharks! Visit the Hammerhead Shark exhibit at Adventure Aquarium to see one up close!

DID YOU KNOW?

A shark's skeleton isn't made of bone. It's made of a softer, more flexible cartilage—the same that is in our ears and nose. Sharks can have as many as seven or more complete rows of teeth in their mouth at any one time, although only one or two rows are functional. They may go through 30,000 teeth in a lifetime. That's why fossilized shark teeth are so common.

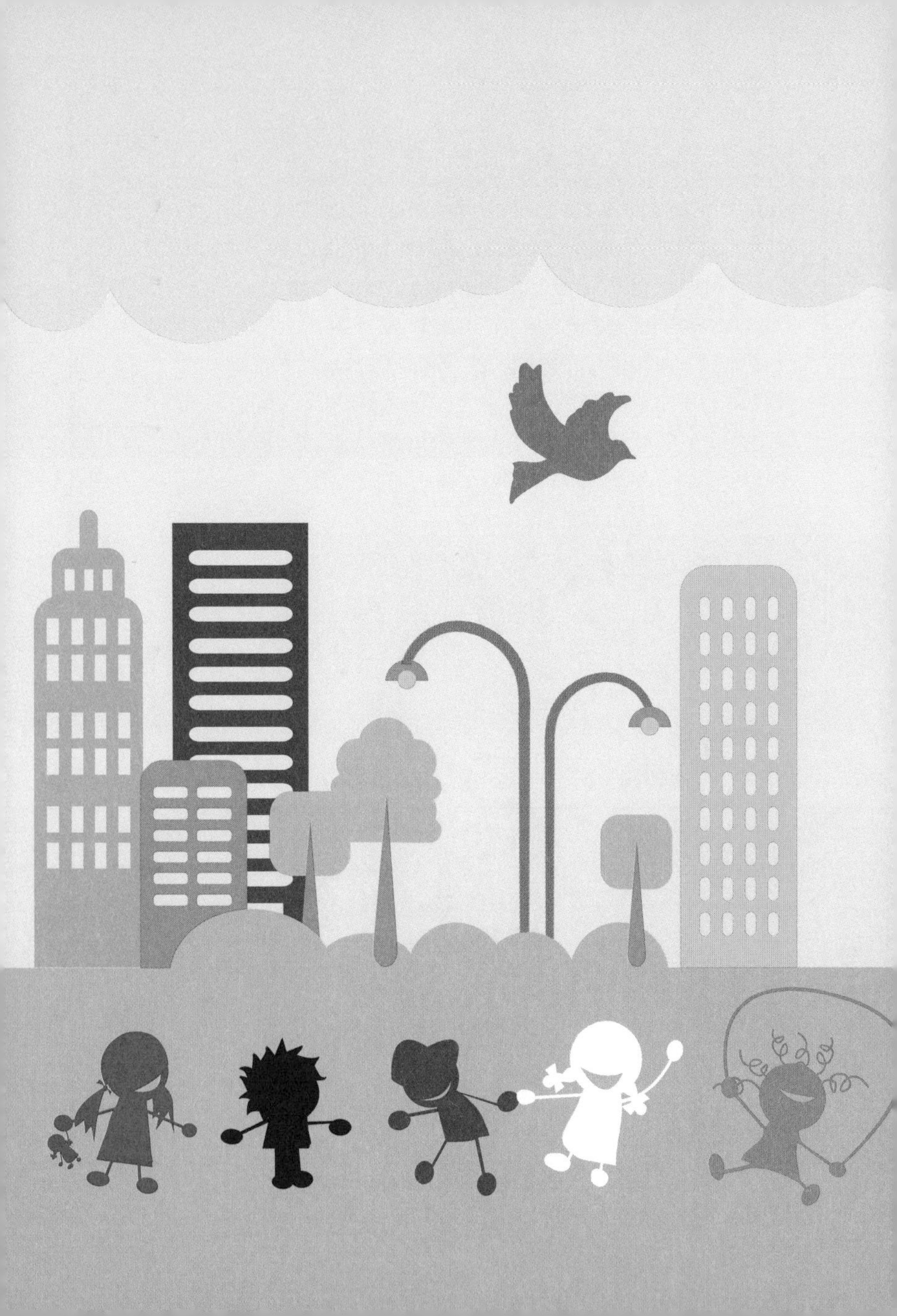

7
Murals, Monet, Giant Sculptures & Rocky

Ready to take an imaginary trip?

Look around the gallery you're in at the famous Philadelphia Museum of Art (2600 Benjamin Franklin Pkwy.; 215-763-8100; philamuseum.org). Pick out your favorite painting. Maybe there is one with kids. Maybe one where people are having fun at the beach.

There are many Impressionist paintings here and the Impressionists were famous for painting everyday scenes. Now close your eyes and imagine you can jump into the painting.

What do you see? What do you hear? What are you doing? What are you wearing?

DID YOU KNOW?

The 72 steps up to the front entrance of the Philadelphia Museum of Art are now called the **Rocky Steps**, after the fictional movie character Rocky Balboa. Sylvester Stallone played Rocky in the popular movie franchise about a boxer who beats the odds to become a champion. The famous scene features Stallone running up the steps in a montage while "Eye of the Tiger" plays. Today, lots of people do the same thing—and then take a selfie down below at the Rocky statue.

DID YOU KNOW?

Julian Abele designed the Philadelphia Museum of Art. He was the first African American architect to design a major museum in the US, and the first African American graduate of the University of Pennsylvania School of Architecture.

The Philadelphia Museum of Art is huge, it has 200 galleries! It's one of the country's oldest public art museums and has some of the greatest collections of American, Asian, and European art anywhere.

You can't see it all, so before you visit talk to your family about what interests you most. Choose a few galleries at which to spend your time.

For sure you'll want to go outside to see the big sculpture garden. Don't miss the great *Giant Three-Way Plug* by Claes Oldenburg, the *Bronze Bell* by Toshiko Takaezu, and the sculpture of a whale's tale by Gordon Gund.

DID YOU KNOW?

The **Rodin Museum** has more sculptures by Auguste Rodin than anywhere outside of Paris. Rodin was a French sculptor, one of the greatest ever, who introduced practices and ideas that inspired modern sculptors. But he was criticized a lot during his lifetime because his work was much more realistic than was popular.

If you like photography and fashion, you'll also want to visit the Perelman Building, it's a short walk from the main building. You'll find modern art here, too.

The Rodin Museum (2151 Benjamin Franklin Pkwy.; 215-763-8100; rodinmuseum.org) is also on the Benjamin Franklin Parkway and part of the Philadelphia Museum of Art. You'll see lots of big sculptures here made from bronze, marble, and plaster. Have you ever tried to make a sculpture?

You can tour most of it in a half hour but if the weather is good, you'll want to spend some time in the garden.

At the Philadelphia Museum of Art, there are lots of free audio guides to different exhibits—you can learn more about armor, for example, or how American families once lived. In the Historic America gallery, the paintings and furniture show you how different life once was.

Travel around the world as you explore different galleries—from the US to Japan and China, Italy and France. Did you see van Gogh's famous *Sunflowers*?

How about the paintings of mothers and children by Mary Cassatt? She was from Pennsylvania but lived most of her life in France. There weren't many successful women artists like her when she lived in the 19th century.

What did you think of Picasso's *Three Musicians*? It's huge and not realistic at all!

Count how many countries the art you've seen comes from. The best part about visiting an art museum—there's no right or wrong way to feel about what you've seen. Everyone will see something different in each work of art.

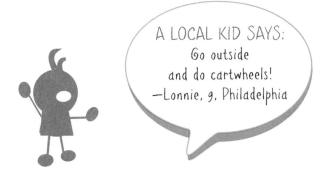

A LOCAL KID SAYS:
Go outside
and do cartwheels!
—Lonnie, 9, Philadelphia

WHAT'S COOL? **The Colored Girls Museum** (4613 Newhall St.; 267-630-4438; thecoloredgirlsmuseum.com) in a three-story house is dedicated to art made by African American women and girls.

What's Impressionism?

Are you an Impressionist?

You don't have to paint a picture of exactly what you are seeing but instead, an "impression" of what that person or landscape looked like—as if we were seeing it in our own eyes—ordinary people sweeping or even taking a bath. And if you were painting a landscape, you'd want to paint outside, looking at how light and color changed the scene. Don't be afraid to use thick and messy brush strokes.

In the late 1800s, a group of artists in France—Claude Monet, Camille Pissarro, Alfred Sisley, Auguste Renoir, Edgar Degas, among them—started painting this way. At first, a lot of people didn't like what they did. They thought their paintings were messy and should have more fancy subjects.

But the impressionists and those who followed changed art forever and inspired artists—including young ones like you—all over the world.

You'll see a lot of their work at the **Philadelphia Museum of Art** (2600 Benjamin Franklin Pkwy.; 215-763-8100; philamuseum.org) and the **Barnes Foundation** (2025 Benjamin Franklin Pkwy.; 215-278-7000; barnesfoundation .org). The Barnes Foundation has the largest group of works by Pierre-Auguste Renoir and Paul Cezanne in the country.

What's your favorite?

Who Was Albert Barnes?

Dr. Albert Barnes grew up poor, but he was really smart—smart enough to win scholarships to college and medical school. He got very rich by inventing an antiseptic.

Once he could, Dr. Barnes began collecting a lot of art and putting it in a specially designed gallery that he built next to his house outside of Philadelphia. He believed art could transform lives. He didn't think it mattered if you knew much about art to enjoy it.

Today, the **Barnes Foundation** (2025 Benjamin Franklin Pkwy.; 215-278-7000; barnesfoundation.org) is in a state-of-the-art building on Benjamin Franklin Parkway near the Philadelphia Museum of Art. The art—there are more than 3,000 works—is arranged the way it was in Dr. Barnes' original gallery.

There are also African sculpture and masks, Native American jewelry and ceramics, Asian paintings and prints, ancient Egyptian art, and more.

Even if you don't know much about art, you'll recognize a lot of the artists' names—Pablo Picasso, Henri Matisse, Pierre-Auguste Renoir.

And if you are lucky, you may see artists around working at the museum. What would you ask them?

A Lot More Than a Road

All along the diagonal **Benjamin Franklin Parkway** are fountains, parks, statues, monuments, an outdoor sculpture garden, and the city's most important museums. Among them are the Philadelphia Museum of Art and the Barnes Foundation, the Rodin Museum, The Franklin Institute, and the Academy of Natural Sciences of Drexel University.

There is public art all along the way too, including Robert Indiana's famous LOVE sculpture, Philadelphia's version of Auguste Rodin's famous *Thinker,* everything from statues and monuments to war heroes to huge abstract works. Can you figure out what the artist was trying to say?

DID YOU KNOW?

There are more than 4,000 murals in Philadelphia during **Mural Arts Month** (muralarts.org). Each October, the city honors the works of public art with trolley tours of neighborhood gardens, mosaics, and a lineup of free and pay-what-you-wish events.

It's only a little more than a mile to walk the whole way. Download the **Museum Without Walls** free audio guide mobile app that will tell you a short story about each sculpture (associationforpublicart.org).

If you are here at the Fourth of July, this is where the city's big concert and fireworks events will be; at Thanksgiving, come for the Thanksgiving Day Parade!

When the weather is warm, kids like to jump in the fountains at **Sister Cities Park** (18th Street and Benjamin Franklin Parkway; 215-440-5500; centercityphila.org/parks/sister-cities-park).

Is it time to get wet?

WHAT'S COOL? **Philadelphia's Magic Gardens** (1020 South St.; 215-733-0390; philadelphiasmagicgardens.org), street-side mosaics that span a half a city block made with mirror, tile, and reclaimed materials.

TELL THE ADULTS

Visiting an art museum can be an adventure— and overwhelming. Many museums, such as the **Philadelphia Museum of Art** (2600 Benjamin Franklin Pkwy.; 215-763-8100; philamuseum.org), have special family exhibit guides, workshops, and audio guides.

Take a virtual tour together before you visit to decide what everyone most wants to see. Check the museum calendar online and, if possible, come when there is a special family program.

Every Wednesday night beginning at 5 p.m., you can "pay what you wish" for access to the entire main building. There are special hands-on activities and performances the first Sunday of the month and admission is free. There are special programs for homeschool families from October to June.

WHAT'S COOL? Exploring an art museum in a new way. Have a scavenger hunt and search for faces, crowns, animals, or shapes. Bring along sketch pads and sketch what you see. Check to see if there are special kids' activities.

Guests also pay what they wish to explore the **Rodin Museum** (2151 Benjamin Franklin Pkwy.; 215-763-8100; rodinmuseum.org) and its gardens.

At the **Barnes Foundation** (2025 Benjamin Franklin Pkwy.; 215-278-7000; barnesfoundation.org), there are PECO Free First Sunday Family Days with special family programming. You can also arrange a special docent tour for your family any day of the week (except Tuesday when the Barnes is closed).

Museum educators offer these tips to get the most out of your visit: Leave when the kids and you have had enough. But afterward, talk about what you've seen—what was everyone's favorite?

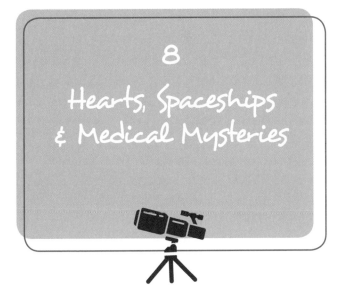

8

Hearts, Spaceships
& Medical Mysteries

Ready to play an important role?

Not as a person, but as something no person can live without—blood pumping through a heart.

Welcome to the Giant Heart at The Franklin Institute (222 N. 20th St.; 215-448-1200; fi.edu). At this exhibit, you move through the chambers of the heart to the lungs as if you were blood. You'll see why this has long been one of the most popular exhibits for kids at a place packed with fun things to do.

Check out the genuine moon rock at the Space Command exhibit where you can spin a ball into the Gravity Well, touch a meteorite that's more than 50 million years old, see the live data coming from the International Space Station, and construct a Mars Rover using K'NEX, or design a rover and see how it does on rugged terrain.

{ WHAT'S COOL? The **Escape Rooms** (fi.edu/escaperooms) at The Franklin Institute, where you are transported to fantastical worlds.

A LOCAL KID SAYS:
If you are visiting for the first time, go to The Franklin Institute. It tells you a lot of Pennsylvania history! My favorite exhibit is the one about electricity!
—Antoine, 10, Philadelphia

See the Maillardet Automaton that inspired the film *Hugo* at the Amazing Machine where you can try being a crane operator; find out what makes an antique sewing machine work; see the inside of a 6-foot clock; and create your own machine using gears, linkages, and pulleys.

Make a paper whirligig, wear wings, and stand in front of a giant fan. Do you feel the lift force? Explore the stories and artifacts from the earliest aviation pioneers and take a virtual reality ride to the moon. Feel motion sick?

Explore the science of sports in the SportsZone, where you can figure out how much energy you need based on your activity level and your body; consider the best drinks for before, during, and after exercise; race a virtual bike course; analyze and improve your pitching; see how well you can balance on a surfboard; and lots more!

DID YOU KNOW?

Your brain weighs just 3 pounds but controls everything that goes on in your body. It's always changing as it makes sense of the world around you. Don't miss the **Your Brain** exhibit at The Franklin Institute.

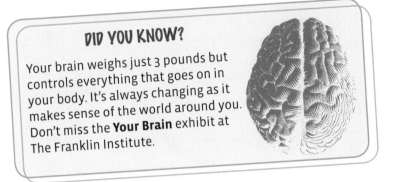

See how and why your brain is always changing at Your Brain, The Franklin Institute's largest exhibit. Fire a model neuron to see how brain cells use chemical and electrical signals, "process" a street scene, and think about how you think.

Explore how the changing earth and climate change will impact everyone's lives. Calculate your carbon footprint. Construct a building to see if it can withstand an earthquake. Deliver your own weather forecast.

Kids also love climbing aboard the giant steam locomotive in the simulated train factory, and exploring

WHAT'S COOL? **Philadelphia Science Festival** (271 N. 21st St.; 215-448-1200; philasciencefestival.org), held every spring with hands-on events for kids and a carnival that helps you see all the science we use every day.

electricity, where you can feel the electricity required for different kinds of light bulbs and learn how electricity is created.

At the Fels Planetarium, the 60-foot-wide immersive dome is the place to explore space with special shows and see what the night sky might look like without any lights or pollution. Go up to the roof outside and see what's happening at the Joel N. Bloom Observatory.

Ready for the "playground of experimentation"? Head to Sir Isaac's Loft, named of course for Sir Isaac Newton, where you can build your own domino maze and see what you think of all the optical illusions. Don't miss the George Rhoads kinetic sculpture—it uses 18 smaller devices to circulate dozens of balls.

Wow!

DID YOU KNOW?

There are many scientists who work and do research at The Franklin Institute. You might meet them during a special program, such as the **Night Skies in the Observatory** (fi.edu/special-events/night-skies-in-the-joel-n-bloom-observatory) led by the institute's chief astronomer. Look through giant telescopes to see stars and planets in the night sky!

Mummies, Bugs, Fossils & Butterflies

You'll find plenty to explore about a lot of different subjects, whether something you know a lot about or something you want to learn more about, at Philadelphia's science museums.

- **Penn Museum** (3260 South St.; 215-898-4000; penn .museum) offers mummies and treasures from 4,500-year old royal tombs as well as the Penn Museum's Warden Garden, with its koi pool and lawns to play on.

- **Mütter Museum of The College of Physicians of Philadelphia** (19 S. 22nd St.; 215-560-8564; mutter museum.org) is famous for its thousands of strange medical specimens, including pieces of Albert Einstein's brain. The collections are still used today to advance medical science.

A LOCAL KID SAYS:
I like the sky show at The Franklin Institute.
—Mary, 10, Philadelphia

WHAT'S COOL? The multimedia show that explores Benjamin Franklin's life and his impact on the world long after he died. Take a selfie with Ben at the giant statue on The Franklin Institute rotunda.

DID YOU KNOW?

Butterflies only live for one to two weeks. You can see many of them at the **Philadelphia Insectarium and Butterfly Pavilion** and **The Academy of Natural Sciences of Drexel University** (1900 Benjamin Franklin Pkwy.; 215-299-1000; ansp.org).

- **Philadelphia Insectarium and Butterfly Pavilion** (8046 Frankford Ave.; 215-335-9500; phillybutterflypavilion.com) has all kinds of bugs and thousands of fluttering butterflies.

- The **Science History Institute** (315 Chestnut St.; 215-925-2222; sciencehistory.org) is the place to see how strange discoveries have changed the way we live and think—even how crayons are colored.

- **The Academy of Natural Sciences of Drexel University** (1900 Benjamin Franklin Pkwy.; 215-299-1000; ansp.org), with its 18 million specimens—is the place for dino lovers and more. There are 18 million plant and animal specimens, a fossil prep lab, and a dig site.

TELL THE ADULTS

Besides Independence National Historical Park, there are many free and nearly free museums and other sites to explore in Philadelphia. The Benjamin Franklin Museum, for one, only costs $5 for adults and $2 for children ages 4 to 16. For kids challenged by too much stimulation, there are Sensory Backpacks available to borrow at no charge with noise-reducing headphones, sunglasses, and weighted toys. Here are some other ideas:

- **American Philosophical Society Museum** (104 S. 5th St.; 215-440-3440; amphilsoc.org/museum)—served as the nation's first "think tank" and has many historic documents.

- **National Museum of American Jewish History** (101 S. Independence Mall East; 215-923-3811; nmajh.org) offers The Only in America Gallery/Hall of Fame, which celebrates the lives and achievements of 20 Jewish Americans, as well as interesting artifacts, including Albert Einstein's pipe and Irving Berlin's piano. Admission is free.

- **Mummers Museum** (1100 S. 2nd St.; 215-336-3050; mummersmuseum.com) celebrates a centuries-old Philadelphia parade whose roots go back to Swedish settlers who brought the Colonies the Christmas custom of dressing in costume and performing pantomimes.

- The **US Mint** (151 N. Independence Mall East; 215-408-0112; usmint.gov) has self-guided tours that include the opportunity to watch coin production from 40 feet above the factory floor and the nation's first coining press. Audio and video stations explain coinage history. Free.

- The **Curtis Institute of Music** (1726 Locust St.; 215-893-5252; curtis.edu) has free concerts on most Monday, Wednesday, and Friday evenings and many weekends during the school year, thanks to the conservatory's gifted students.

- **Macy's** (1300 Market St.; 215-241-9000; visitmacysusa.com) offers free live performances on a 1904 pipe organ with 28,500 pipes. An organist performs 45-minute concerts twice daily.

Please Touch Museum

Who knew you could learn so much by playing?

You can at the **Please Touch Museum** (Memorial Hall, 4231 Avenue of the Republic; 215-581-3181; pleasetouch museum.org) where the exhibits are designed for you to have fun and learn at the same time. This is a great place for little kids, but there is plenty for everyone—including grownups. There's a "Please Touch" garden where you can try to identify herbs by their smell or stroll through the cornstalks and pepper plants. See old-fashioned toys and games kids once played with. Take a ride on the carousel—it's more than 100 years old! Visit the kid-size city or navigate the hedge maze in Wonderland where you'll want to wind through the Hall of Mirrors. Float a boat in River Adventures or invent an ice cream flavor at Road-side Attractions.

There's an Adventure Camp, an Imagination Playground, and plenty of changing exhibits, too.

The best part: Plenty of room to run around and play!

PHILADELPHIA SCAVENGER HUNT

Look carefully throughout Philadelphia for the following things and check off what you find!

- ❏ Giant heart
- ❏ Moon rocks
- ❏ Mummies
- ❏ Steam locomotive
- ❏ Planetarium
- ❏ Butterflies
- ❏ Fossils
- ❏ Tyrannosaurus rex
- ❏ Maillardet automaton

DID YOU KNOW?

The Tyrannosaurus rex was one of the largest predators to ever live. You can see a giant T. rex skeleton as well as many others, dinosaur eggs, footprints, and more at the **Academy of Natural Sciences Dinosaur Hall** (1900 Benjamin Franklin Pkwy.; 215-299-1000; ansp.org).

9
Fun & Games
Outside

Are you up for a challenge?

Treetop Quest (51 Chamounix Dr.; 267-901-4145; treetopquest.com) in West Fairmount Park is a multi–zip line obstacle attraction with more than 60 obstacles—everything from swings, jumps, tightropes, and zip lines—all of varying difficulty.

Lead the way for your family! Go through as many times as you want over 2.5 hours. There's a "Chickpea" course for kids 4 to 6 years old. Don't worry—the staff will make sure you are safely harnessed and know how to work the equipment.

Fairmount Park (Reservoir Drive; visitphilly.com/things-to-do/attractions/fairmount-park) is huge. It has more than 2,000 acres of hills, trails, waterfront, and woods. It's divided into East Park and West Park. You can horseback ride, hike, see a Japanese tea ceremony, or just run around and play. The park is also the summer home for the Philadelphia Orchestra, so there are summer concerts here.

{ WHAT'S COOL? Free outdoor movies at the **Great Plaza at Penn's Landing** (Columbus Boulevard and Chestnut Street; 215-922-2FUN; delawareriverwaterfront.com/events/great-plaza-at-penn-s-landing) Thursday nights in July and August.

The East Park is home to the Philadelphia Art Museum, historic houses, and the Smith Memorial Playground & Playhouse, one of the oldest playgrounds in the country and famous for the Ann Newman Giant Wooden Slide that's more than 110 years old. Jump, swing, climb as much as you like. For kids 5 and under, there's Straz Land.

West Fairmont Park is home to the Please Touch Museum, the Philadelphia Zoo, the Shofuso Japanese House and Garden, Concourse Lake, and much more. Do you like plants and flowers? You'll want to see the greenhouse at the Fairmount Park Horticulture Center (100 N. Horticultural Dr., Philadelphia, PA; 215-685-0096; hortevents.com).

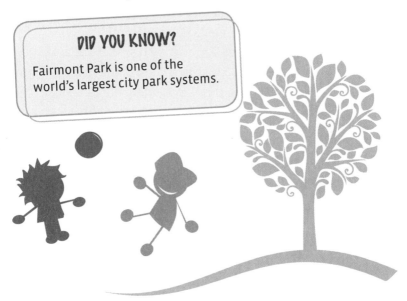

DID YOU KNOW?
Fairmont Park is one of the world's largest city park systems.

DID YOU KNOW?

You can meet Philadelphia artists and see them working in repurposed shipping containers at **The Studios at Cherry Street Pier** (121 N. Columbus Blvd.; 215-923-0818; cherry streetpier.com/space). You can also buy souvenirs from local merchants and artisans at **The Market**.

If you or anyone in your family has special challenges, the Carousel House (4300 Avenue of the Republic; 215-685-0160; carouselhousepa.com) has an accessible garden, playground, picnic area, and even fitness track.

At the Smith Playground (3500 Reservoir Dr.; 215-765-4325; smithplayground.org), younger kids love to play in the big playhouse where they can ride trikes, drive a train, and cook in the kitchen. For children 5 and under, Straz Land features more than 20 pieces of age-appropriate play equipment, and at the 16,000-square-foot play-house, kids run the show.

The best part: You can visit all year and see how nature changes season to season.

Lloyd Hall has an indoor basketball court and this is also the place to rent bikes for a ride on the Schuylkill River Trail (215-568-6002; wheelfunrentals.com/Locations/Philadelphia).

See what programs are going on at the Fairmount Water Works Interpretive Center (640 Waterworks Dr.; 215-685-0723; fairmountwaterworks.org). Learn how river water is turned into safe tap water!

Of course, there are places to play outside all over Philadelphia—more than 300 neighborhood parks, rec centers, and playgrounds. There are more than 400 basketball courts, 5 ice skating rinks, and 74 pools. Check to see if there are special family events in a park when you visit (phila.gov/parksandrecreation).

The only hard part—deciding what you want to do outside!

TELL THE ADULTS

Especially in a big city, it is easy for families to get separated. Make sure the kids know what to do if this happens, whether you are in a museum or at the Delaware River Waterfront:

- Play the "what if" game. What if they can't find you? They need to look for someone in an official uniform—a police officer or security guard, or an employee at the museum or park who can call security. They need to explain that they can't find you.

- If they don't have their own phone, make sure they have your cell phone numbers written. They

A LOCAL KID SAYS:
Get a Phillies hat
for a souvenir.
—Mary, 10, Philadelphia

also need to know where you are staying and the address. Kids, like adults, can get rattled in stressful situations so it is wise to have all the information written down on a card in their pocket—including your names. Sometimes when asked their parents' names young children will just say, "Mom" and "Dad."

- Remind them never to go off with a stranger, no matter how nice that stranger may seem.

- They should remain as close as possible to where you were last together so you can double back to find them.

{ **WHAT'S COOL?** PopUp Play at the **Spruce Street Harbor Park** with special kid-friendly activities. Events are held Sunday from the end of May until the end of September at the **Delaware River Waterfront** (121 N. Columbus Blvd.; 215-922-2FUN; delawareriverwaterfront.com).

The Most Fun Waterfront

Have you ever seen a pop-up park? Spring through fall, the **Spruce Street Harbor Park** on the **Delaware River Waterfront** (121 N. Columbus Blvd.; 215-922-2FUN; delawareriverwaterfront.com) has tree-slung hammocks, cargo container arcades, and plenty of good eats.

The **Blue Cross RiverRink Summerfest** (101 S. Columbus Rd.; 215-925-RINK; delawareriverwaterfront.com/places/blue-cross-riverrink-summerfest) has an outdoor roller-skating rink, Ferris wheel, carousel, mini golf, arcade games, and more.

Winterfest (delawareriverwaterfront.com/places/blue-cross-riverrink-winterfest) is where you can ice skate outside and come for special holiday celebrations, fire pits, indoor games, and hot drinks.

The **Great Plaza at Penn's Landing** (Columbus Boulevard and Chestnut Street; 215-922-2FUN; delaware riverwaterfront.com/events/great-plaza-at-penn-s-landing), next to Blue Cross RiverRink, is where you'll find concerts and festivals in spring, summer, and fall. There are festivals that celebrate all different cultures—Irish, African American, India, Caribbean, Mexican, and more.

Washington Avenue Pier (S. Christopher Columbus Blvd.; washingtonavenuegreen.com), formerly named Pier 53, was once an immigration station. Today it is the place to go to reach out and touch the water. The elevated boardwalk lets you see the wetlands below. Climb the spiral staircase for great views of the Delaware River, Center City, and the Benjamin Franklin and Walt Whitman bridges.

You can canoe, kayak, or take a ride in a swan boat at **Penn's Landing Marina** (301 S. Christopher Columbus Blvd.; 215-928-8803; delawareriverwaterfront.com/places/marina -at-penn-s-landing). There are also various cruises from here— including rides across the Delaware River in the summer on the **RiverLink Ferry** (Columbus Boulevard and Walnut Street; 856-964-5465; delawareriverwaterfront.com/places/riverlink -ferry), which can take you to Adventure Aquarium or the Battleship New Jersey Museum and Memorial.

Want to hear the wildlife splash into the water? You can at **Race Street Pier** (Race Street and North Christopher Columbus Boulevard; 215-922-2FUN; delawareriverwaterfront .com/places/race-street-pier/events), where passing boats, runners, and trains often disturb the wildlife that calls the river home.

Bring a picnic—and your pooch!

Ahoy, Sailors!

Do you ever think about joining the Navy?

The Battleship *New Jersey*, which served in World War II and during the Cold War, is the country's most decorated battleship. Now retired and docked in the Delaware River, the battleship is part of the **Battleship New Jersey Museum and Memorial** (62 Battleship Pl., Camden, NJ; 856-966-1652; battleshipnewjersey.org). You can take a tour ride in the 4-D flight simulator, look inside the onboard helicopter, and even have a sleepover in the sailors' bunks as part of the Overnight Encampment program.

See what it was like to serve in the navy throughout history at the **Independence Seaport Museum** (211 S. Columbus Blvd.; 215-413-8655; phillyseaport.org) on the edge of the Delaware River. Explore the Spanish-American War cruiser *Olympia* and World War II submarine *Becuna* docked outside. Climb through a full-size reconstruction of the 1797 schooner *Diligence*. Every Saturday is "Seafarin' Saturday" with special kids' activities.

Play Ball!

Love sports? You're in luck in Philadelphia because whenever you visit, you'll find a sports team to watch:

- **BASEBALL**: The Philadelphia Phillies (Citizens Bank Park, One Citizens Bank Way; 215-463-1000; mlb.com/phillies).

- **SOCCER**: The Philadelphia Union (1 Stadium Dr., Chester, PA [15 miles from Center City]; 610-859-3100; philadelphiaunion.com).

- **FOOTBALL**: The Philadelphia Eagles (Lincoln Financial Field, One Lincoln Financial Field Way; 515-463-5500; philadelphiaeagles.com).

- **BASKETBALL**: The Philadelphia 76ers (Wells Fargo Center, 3601 S. Broad St.; 215-336-3600; nba.com/sixers).

- **ICE HOCKEY**: The Philadelphia Flyers (Wells Fargo Center, 3601 S. Broad St.; 215-336-3600; nhl.com/flyers).

DID YOU KNOW?

Philadelphia is one of just a few cities with five professional sports teams.

The Philadelphia Eagles won the Super Bowl in 2018.

A LOCAL KID SAYS:
My favorite Philadelphia team is the 76ers because I love basketball!
—Shakur, 10, Philadelphia

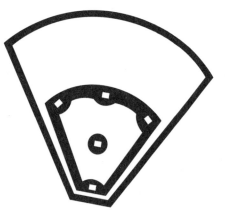

DID YOU KNOW?

A model of the Liberty Bell, 100 feet above street level, rings at Citizens Bank Park after every Phillies home run.

WHAT'S COOL? **The Yard** next to right field—a huge interactive kids' baseball experience at **Citizens Bank Park** (1 Citizens Bank Way; 215-463-1000; mlb.com/phillies/ballpark). Check out the kid-sized portions at the Phood Cart and the Kid's Corner at Citizens Bank Park.

Philadelphia is 1 of 9 cities with 5 professional sports teams (most cities only have 4). Can you match the team with the sport below?

Phillies

76ers

Flyers

Eagles

Union

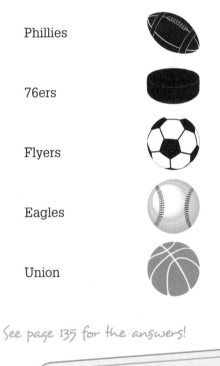

See page 135 for the answers!

DID YOU KNOW?

The 76ers got their name because the Declaration of Independence was signed in 1776.

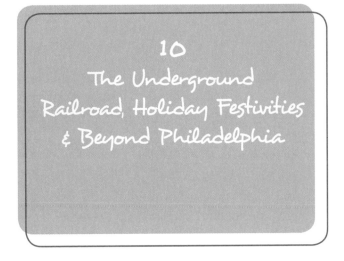

10
The Underground
Railroad, Holiday Festivities
& Beyond Philadelphia

There is so much to explore

outside of Philadelphia as well—such as the Conestoga wagon hanging from the ceiling at the Mercer Museum (84 S. Pine St., Doylestown, PA; 215-345-0210; mercermuseum.org). The Mercer Museum has nearly 50,000 artifacts devoted to early-American working life.

By the end of the 19th century, handmade things were considered less valuable as people began to prefer new machine-made goods. Archeologist and historian Henry Mercer decided to preserve some of those hand-made goods from everyday life in the 18th and 19th centuries—everything from hand tools to horse-drawn vehicles. There's even an Animals on the Loose exhibit with animal-shaped objects in the hands-on children's gallery. The Imagination Gallery offers family activities.

DID YOU KNOW?

One of the country's most popular haunted places is in Philadelphia at the **Eastern State Penitentiary** (2027 Fairmont Ave.; 215-236-3300; easternstate .org), an abandoned prison. Visit during the end of September through early November—if you dare!

A mile from the museum, Mercer built a six-story concrete building named Fonthill Castle to hold this collection. Today, the castle is a National Historic Landmark and there are special events during the year for kids—like the annual Kite Day.

Like to see old-fashioned toys? Then you'll love the American Treasure Tour (1 American Treasure Way, Oaks, PA; 866-970-8687; americantreasuretour .com) next to Valley Forge National Monument. The old tire factory is packed with everything from a giant popsicle stick castle, clowns, dollhouses, music boxes, and one of the world's largest collections of mechanical music. It's only open Thursday through Sunday, so plan ahead.

Pick your own fruit at Linvilla Orchards (137 W. Knowlton Rd., Media, PA; 610-876-7116; linvilla.com), a 300-acre farm where you can also take a hayride and explore the garden center.

If you like art, come on the first Sunday of the month for special kids' activities at the Brandywine River Museum of Art (1 Hoffman's Mill Rd., Chadds Ford, PA; 610-388-2700;

DID YOU KNOW?

There are two New Year's Eve fireworks displays in Philadelphia on the **Waterfront over the Delaware River** (121 N. Columbus Blvd.; 215-922-2FUN; delaware riverwaterfront.com)—one at 6 p.m. for families, and a second at midnight.

brandywine.org) that is focused on American artists. Take a walk outside through wetlands that are maintained especially so that you can explore there.

Stop for s'mores and pancakes at the Bittersweet Kitchen (18 S. Orange St., Media, PA; 610-566-1660; eatatbittersweet.com), where you can borrow toys while you are waiting for your food.

Of course, there are lots of Revolutionary War sites outside of Philadelphia, including Valley Forge, where George Washington whipped the ragtag Continental army into shape, and different battlefields such as the Paoli Battlefield (Monument and Wayne Avenues, Malvern, PA; 484-320-7173; pbpfinc.org), the site of a bloody battle in which many lives were lost in 1777. Today you can see cannons, historical obstacles, and more.

Visit farm animals and learn what farm life would have been like at the time of the Revolutionary War at the Peter Wentz Farmstead (2030 Shearer Rd., Lansdale, PA; 610-584-5104; peterwentzfarmsteadsociety .org). George Washington used this farm as a temporary headquarters in the fall of 1777.

Where will you go first?

A LOCAL KID SAYS:
Philly is a great place! Get a Philly Snow Globe for a souvenir and have a great visit!
—Naomi, 10, Philadelphia

{ **WHAT'S COOL?** **The Indoor Children's Garden at Longwood Gardens** (1001 Longwood Rd., Kennett Square, PA; 610-388-1000; longwoodgardens.org), with hands-on water features and secret stairways. In summer, splash in the Flower Fountain outside. Come in October for the Pumpkin Playground! And the mums are shaped into everything from clouds to pagodas.

If anyone in your family has physical or mental challenges, be sure to check out visitphilly.com/accessibility. The site points users to the best ways to enjoy Philadelphia and the special resources available.

If you have young children in the group, consider a visit to **Sesame Place** (100 Sesame Rd., Langhorne, PA; 215-702-ELMO; sesameplace.com), the only theme park in the nation based entirely on the long-running children's television show. A popular water park (open Memorial Day through Labor Day), rides, interactive activities, parades, fireworks, and shows add to the fun. Older kids will have fun watching the little ones—and remembering when they were fans.

DID YOU KNOW?

In Philadelphia, "Yo!" is a greeting used to get someone's attention, "gravy" is red pasta sauce, and "Wawa" is a chain of Philadelphia area convenience stores.

WHAT'S COOL? **Peddler's Village** (Routes 202 and 263, Lahaska, PA; 215-794-4000; peddlersvillage.com) in Bucks County with Giggleberry Mountain, the area's largest indoor obstacle course. Peddler's Village also offers lots of seasonal festivals, including a 6-week Scarecrow Festival where you can learn how to make a scarecrow.

Everyone will enjoy the indoor **LEGOLAND Discovery Center** (Plymouth Meeting Mall, 500 W. Germantown Pike, Plymouth Meeting, PA; 267-245-9696; legolanddiscoverycenter.com)– complete with a LEGO-themed ride, 4-D cinema, and 10 play areas, including a DUPLO Park for the toddler set. An onsite cafe and store ensure everybody walks away satisfied.

Another good bet for all ages outside of Philadelphia is the **American Helicopter Museum & Education Center** (1220 American Blvd., West Chester, PA; 610-436-9600; americanhelicopter .museum), with more than 35 civilian and military helicopters and kids' play area with puzzles, toys, and the chance to "build" a helicopter. Several times a year and during special events, guests of all ages have a chance to ride in a helicopter.

The Underground Railroad

During the time of slavery, brave people would hide escaped slaves as they made their way north to freedom. Philadelphians were very active in the abolitionist movement against slavery.

If you want to learn more about the **Underground Railroad** (which wasn't really a railroad at all) you can pick up a brochure of the key historical attractions at the Independence Visitor Center (599 Market St., 1 N. Independence Mall West; 800-537-7676; phlvisitorcenter.com) and the African American Museum (701 Arch St.; 215-574-0380; aampmuseum.org), or you can download it at visitphilly.com/underground-railroad-in -philadelphia. Among the sites you will want to visit:

DID YOU KNOW?

There is an **African American Children's Book Fair** (theafricanamericanchildrensbookproject.org) every winter with fun activities that encourage kids to read. This event is open to the public and all are welcome.

- **Mother Bethel A.M.E. Church** (419 S. 6th St.; visitphilly
  .com/things-to-do/attractions/mother-bethel-african
  -methodist-episcopal-ame-church) is the active flagship
  of the nation's first African American denomination where
  fugitive slaves sought refuge.

- **Bucks County Underground Railroad Trail** (150 Basin
  Park, Bristol, PA; visitbuckscounty.com/things-to-do/planning
  -ideas/underground-railroad) is a miles-long, driveable trail
  that includes taverns, churches, private residences, and a
  waterfront memorial to Harriet Tubman. Trace the paths of
  escaped slaves as they sought refuge in the North.

- **Belmont Mansion** (2000 Belmont Mansion Dr., Fairmount
  Park; 215-878-8844; belmontmansion.org) was built by
  William Peters in 1742 and was later home to his son, Judge
  Richard Peters. Judge Peters was a slaveholder but allowed
  some African Americans to buy their freedom. He also
  allowed runaway slaves to hide in the mansion's attic and
  cellar. There is an Underground Railroad Museum on site.

DID YOU KNOW?

Harriet Tubman, who was born into slavery and
escaped to freedom in Pennsylvania, became a leading
abolitionist fighting against slavery, leading others to
freedom in Philadelphia. She was also a nurse and a
Union spy during the Civil War.

Holiday Happenings

You're guaranteed a fun time if you visit Philadelphia over the holidays. And you can buy some cool holiday gifts, too! It may be cold, but there is so much happening in and around Philadelphia!

- **Thanksgiving Day Parade** along Benjamin Franklin Parkway.

- **Christmas Village in Philadelphia** (1501 John F Kennedy Blvd.; 215-268-7606; philachristmas.com). This German-style market at LOVE Park (the official name is the John F. Kennedy Plaza) features more than 80 booths selling everything from ornaments to warm hats and plenty of treats to eat. Open from late November through Christmas Eve.

- **Longwood Gardens Christmas** (1001 Longwood Rd., Kennett Square, PA; 610-388-1000; longwoodgardens.org). Thousands of poinsettias and Christmas trees transform the indoor gardens, where concerts take place daily. Outside, 500,000 lights glitter in the trees, and fountains dance to seasonal music. Open mid-November through early January.

- The **Franklin Square Holiday Festival** (6th and Race Streets; 215-629-4026; historicphiladelphia.org) features the **Electrical Spectacle: A Holiday Light Show**. Electric company PECO aptly presents the illumination of Franklin Square, while the square itself offers hot drinks and festive snacks. Open in November and December.

- **The Rothman Ice Rink and Wintergarden** (1 S. 15th St.; 215-440-5500; visitphilly.com/things-to-do/attractions/the-rothman-ice-rink-at-dilworth-park) return to Dilworth Park from November through February.

- **Blue Cross RiverRink Winterfest** (101 S. Columbus Blvd.; 215-629-3200; delawareriverwaterfront.com/places/blue-cross-riverrink-winterfest). The ice rink and Winterfest wonderland return to Penn's Landing November through March, complete with a lodge, arcade, and confectionery cabin.

- **Macy's Christmas Light Show** (1300 Market St.; 215-241-9000; l.macys.com/philadelphia-pa). The Grand Court of the historic Wanamaker department store (now Macy's) offers a free show of dancing lights set to the famed Wanamaker Organ. There are performances every two hours during store hours throughout the holiday season.

- **A Philly Pops Christmas**: Spectacular Sounds of the Season! The Philly POPS' Festival Chorus, The Philadelphia Boys Choir, and the St. Thomas Gospel Choir get everyone in the holiday spirit with their concerts each December (Kimmel Center, 300 S. Broad St.; 215-893-1999; phillypops.org).

- **Washington Crossing The Delaware River**. Each Christmas day, "General Washington" (an actor dressed as the Founding Father) leads a surprise attack on the British during this annual re-enactment—complete with army uniforms, games, and other activities—at Washington Crossing Historic Park (1112 River Rd., Washington Crossing, PA; 215-493-4076; washingtoncrossingpark.org).

SECRET WORD PUZZLE

Using the key, write the letters under the symbols to figure out the secret phrase. Clue: Harriet Tubman escaped to freedom on this trail.

For example: 🚲 🏞️ 🛤️ ✈️ = b i r d

[puzzle symbols]

___ _____

_____

a= ✔	b= 🚲	c= 🏙️	d= ✈️	e= 🎁
f= 🏭	g= 🏛️	h= 🏠	i= 🏞️	j= 🏚️
k= 🐝	l= ?	m= ❗	n= 👁️	o= 🚢
p= 🛤️	q= ⛺	r= 🛤️	s= ✦	t= ✉️
u= 📢	v= 🔷	w= 🚩	x= 🔊	y= ❤️
z= 🌿	.= ◼️	!= 🚌	,= 🌶️	

See page 135 for the answer key.

Now try and make your own secret messages in the space below.

What A Trip!

I came to Philadelphia with:

_____

_____

_____

The weather was:

_____

_____

_____

We went to:

_____

_____

_____

We ate:

_____

_____

_____

We bought:

_____

_____

I saw these famous Philadelphia sites:

_____

_____

_____

My favorite thing about Philadelphia was:

_____

_____

_____

My best memory of Philadelphia was:

_____

_____

_____

My favorite souvenir is:

_____

_____

_____

WHAT DID YOU SEE?

We bet you had a great time in Philadelphia! Draw some pictures or paste in some photos of your trip!

Answer Keys

Welcome to Philadelphia (p. 11)

Benjamin Franklin
(7)

Elfreth's Alley
(5)

Logan Square
(3)

The Philadelphia Tribune
(4)

William Penn
(6)

Delaware River Waterfront
(9)

Fairmount Park
(2)

Center City
(8)

Betsy Ross
(1)

Answer:

B   R   O   T   H   E   R   L   Y   L   O   V   E

(1) (2) (3) (4) (5) (6) (2) (7) (8)   (7) (3) (9) (6)

Secret Code (p. 23)

"A true friend is the best possession."

Philadelphia Word Scramble (p. 35)

Benjamin Franklin

Roger Sherman

Thomas Jefferson

John Adams

George Washington

John Hancock

Crossing the Delaware (p. 49)

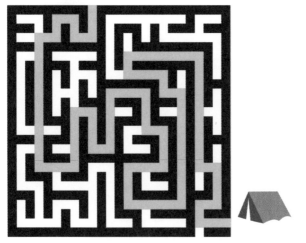

Match the Team with the Sport (p. 113)

Phillies	Baseball
76ers	Basketball
Flyers	Hockey
Eagles	Football
Union	Soccer

Secret Word Puzzle (p. 126)

The Underground Railroad

Index

About the Author

Award-winning author Eileen Ogintz is a leading national family travel expert whose syndicated "Taking the Kids" is the most widely distributed column in the country on family travel. She has also created TakingtheKids.com, which helps families make the most of their vacations together. Ogintz is the author of seven family travel books and is often quoted in major publications such as *USA Today*, the *Wall Street Journal*, and the *New York Times*, as well as parenting and women's magazines on family travel. She has appeared on such television programs as *The Today Show*, *Good Morning America*, and *The Oprah Winfrey Show*, as well as dozens of local radio and television news programs. She has traveled around the world with her three children and others in the family, talking to traveling families wherever she goes. She is also the author of *The Kid's Guide to New York City*, *The Kid's Guide to Orlando*, *The Kid's Guide to Washington, DC*, *The Kid's Guide to Chicago*, *The Kid's Guide to Denver, Boulder & Colorado Ski Country*, *The Kid's Guide to Los Angeles County*, *The Kid's Guide to San Diego*, *The Kid's Guide to San Francisco*, *The Kid's Guide to the Great Smoky Mountains*, *The Kid's Guide to Boston* (all Globe Pequot), *The Kid's Guide to Maine*, and *The Kid's Guide to Acadia National Park* (Down East Books).